Planetariums

Jennifer B. Gillis

Rourke

Publishing LLC
Vero Beach, Florida 32964

www.rourkepublishing.com

PHOTO CREDITS: All photos © Chabot Space and Science Center, except pg.11 © eromaze; pg.14 © Austin Peay State University; pg.16 © Manfred Konrad; pg.17 © Magali Bolla; pg.19 © UCLA Planetarium; pg.21 © Learning Technologies, Inc.

Editor: Robert Stengard-Olliges

Cover design by Michelle Moore.

imprint
TK

Dedication: The publisher wishes to thank Karen Kornegay and Mickey Jo Sorrel at the Morehead Planetarium, University of North Carolina at Chapel Hill, and Ralph White at SciWorks Planetarium in Winston-Salem, North Carolina, for their expertise in the preparation of this book.

Library of Congress Cataloging-in-Publication Data

Gillis, Jennifer Blizin, 1950-
 Planetariums / Jennifer Blizin Gillis.
     p. cm. -- (Field trips)
 Includes index.
 ISBN 978-1-60044-562-0
 1. Planetariums--Juvenile literature. I. Title.
 QB70 .G55 2008
 520.74 22
                                        2007017257

Printed in the USA

CG/CG

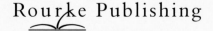

Rourke Publishing

www.rourkepublishing.com – rourke@rourkepublishing.com
Post Office Box 3328. Vero Beach. FL 32964

Table of Contents

A Trip to Space

Look up at the night sky. Do you wonder what is up there? On a field trip to a planetarium, you can travel to the stars while you sit in your seat. Planetariums are special theaters where you can learn about stars, planets, and **constellations**.

▲
Constellation effects at the Ask Jeeves
Planetarium in San Francisco, California.

Before the Show

There may be some **exhibits** to look at. Some planetariums have pictures of stars and planets taken with powerful telescopes on Earth. You may also see pictures that were taken by spaceships. Sometimes there are models that show what planets might look like if you could see them close up.

▲

Mars Encounter exhibit at the Chabot Space and Science Center.

Who Will You Meet?

An **educator** may show you the exhibits and tell you about the planetarium. A **technician** may run the machines inside the theater. At some large planetariums you may get to meet an **astronomer**. Astronomers are scientists who study stars and planets. People who work in planetariums need to know a lot about stars and space.

▲

This large telescope, named Rachel is open to
the public and scientists.

In the Star Theater

Walking into a star theater may make you think of going to the movies. The theater will be almost dark. Soft music may be playing. The seats are just like the ones in a movie theater, too. Now, look up. In most star theaters the ceiling is a high, round **dome** with just a few lights showing at the edges. It looks like a round movie screen in the soft light.

▲

An audio-visual system controls the background
lights and music in the dark dome.

The Star Projector

In many planetariums a large machine stands near the front or in the middle of the room. You may think it's a strange insect or a creature from outer space. This is the star **projector**. One end is shaped like a ball with many holes in it. Inside, a powerful light will shine to project—or throw—the shapes of the stars onto the dome.

▲
A star projector makes the stars inside a
planetarium.

Seeing Stars

Slowly, the theater gets darker. All of a sudden you are looking into a starry night sky. The star projector twists and rolls to make the stars move across the dome. This makes it feel like the room is spinning, but it isn't. You are safe in your seat.

Seeing stars at the Robert Sears Planetarium ▶ in Clarksville, Tennessee.

Outside and Inside

There are millions of stars in the real night sky, but you could never see them all. You might be able to see the planets Mercury, Venus, Mars, Jupiter, and Saturn—but only as tiny specks. In a planetarium you can see more than 2,000 stars, the constellations, all the planets, and their moons. You can see how they move in their **orbits** around the sun.

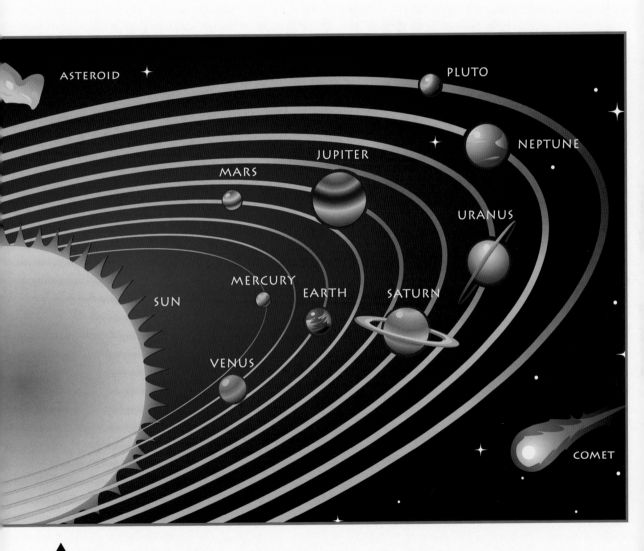

ASTEROID

PLUTO

NEPTUNE

JUPITER

MARS

URANUS

MERCURY

EARTH

SATURN

SUN

VENUS

COMET

▲

Planets and other space objects orbit around the sun. Did you know that Pluto is no longer a planet?

Behind the Scenes

What does it take to make the inside of a building look like outer space? It takes projectors, computers, and lots of light bulbs! Technicians write programs for the computers. These programs tell the projectors what to show and when to move. It can take as long as a year to write a program for a planetarium show. Technicians also have to keep the projectors running. Bulbs and parts for star projectors can cost thousands of dollars.

▲
The control console at the UCLA Planetarium.

Traveling Planetariums

If you can't get to a planetarium, a planetarium might come to you. Many planetariums visit schools with traveling planetariums. A traveling planetarium looks like a giant silver beach ball. A fan moves air through a tube to blow it up. You crawl inside through another tube. Inside, a small star projector shows the night sky.

▲

The STARLAB planetarium can
move from school to school.

Did You Know?

- The dome inside a planetarium looks thick and solid. But if you could see it up close you would notice that it is really a thin metal frame with thousands of tiny holes in it.

- Star projectors in planetariums can show what the night sky looks like anywhere in the world on any date. They can show how the sky looked as far back and as far ahead as 5,000 years. Some projectors can even show how parts of the sky look from other planets.

- The first planetariums were models of the planets moving around the sun, called orreries. They were named for a place in Ireland where one was built in the 1700s. In 1923, the Zeiss factory built the first planetarium in which stars were projected onto a dome.

- Takayuki Ohira, who designed one of the most advanced star projectors in the world, designed a home planetarium for a video game company. The Homestar planetarium is a plastic ball that can project 10,000 stars on your ceiling or walls.

Glossary

astronomer (ah STRON ah mer) — person who studies stars, planets, and space

constellation (kon steh LAY shun) — group of stars that looks somewhat like an animal or an object and is given a special name, such as "the Big Dipper"

dome (dohm) — rounded roof that looks like half of a large ball

educator (EJ you kate r) — person at a museum, planetarium, or other public place that teaches people about the exhibits

exhibit (eg ZIB it) — something put in a place where many people can see it

orbit (OR bit) — path of planets as they move around the sun

projector (pruh JECT er) — machine that directs light through a hole to show pictures on a screen, wall, or ceiling

technician (tek NISH in) — person who is specially trained to do a certain job

Index

Further Reading

Alberti, Theresa. *Out and About at the Planetarium*. Picture Window Books, 2004.

Harris, Nicolas. *Stars and Planets*. Blackbirch Press, 2006.

Prins, M.D. *Paper Galaxy: Out-of-this-World Projects*. Sterling Publishing, 2007.

Websites to Visit

www.haydenplanetarium.org
www.adlerplanetarium.org
www.calacademy.org/planetarium/

About the Author

Jennifer B. Gillis is an author and editor of nonfiction books and poetry for children. A graduate of Gilford College in North Carolina, she has taught foreign language and social studies in North Carolina, Virginia, and Illinois.